Merry Christmas,
Eleanor!
– 2008 –
Love, Dinah

Mrs Cook's

BOOK OF RECIPES

Endpapers: An embroidery worked by Elizabeth Cook, showing the routes her husband took in the Pacific. Collection of the Australian National Maritime Museum

Mrs Cook's

BOOK OF RECIPES

FOR MARINERS IN DISTANT SEAS

JOHN DUNMORE

Quercus

First published in Great Britain in 2007 by

Quercus
21 Bloomsbury Square
London
WC1A 2NS

A CIP catalogue reference for this book is available from
the British Library

ISBN 1 84724 168 9
ISBN-13 978 1 84724 168 9

Printed and bound in Great Britain

10 9 8 7 6 5 4 3 2 1

Contents

A Note on Elizabeth Cook   7

To the Reader   9

Stewed Albatross   14

Beer, Lemon Juice and Other Anti-scorbutic Beverages   19

Biscuits   32

Dog Stewed and in Broth   36

Breadfruit and Suchlike   41

Fish, Fresh and Potted   43

Goat, Roast and Stewed   52

Gruel   57

Rats in Stew   61

Sauerkraut or Pickled Cabbage   64

Turtle Soup   67

To Welcome Home a Weary Mariner: 71

     Yorkshire Pudding   73

     Roast Beef   74

     Fried Celery   75

     Jugged Pigeons   76

     Oyster Loaves   78

     Strawberries as Fritters   79

     Poor Knights Pudding   80

     The Hasty Pudding   82

     Pumpkin Pie   83

Glossary   87

Bibliography   89

A Note on Elizabeth Cook

Elizabeth Batts was born in Wapping High Street, London, on 24 January 1741, the daughter of alehouse keepers. On 21 December 1762, she married a young naval officer named James Cook. He returned to duty in Newfoundland waters in April and eventually carried out the three major expeditions to the Pacific Ocean and around the world that have earned him immortal fame. On 14 February 1779, during the last of these voyages he was killed in Hawaii. He was 50.

Elizabeth Cook lived on until 13 May 1835, having reached the age of 94, something of a record for those times. She outlived not only her husband, but their six children, three of whom died in early childhood, one of scarlet fever in his teens and two while serving in the Navy.

She lived through the reigns of George III and George IV and died during that of William IV. Her lifetime encompassed the War of the Austrian Succession, the Seven Years War, the American War of Independence, and the French Revolutionary and Napoleonic Wars. She witnessed the rapid growth and transformation of London into a large modern city, and the birth of the industrial age.

Shortly after her marriage, she had settled in a terrace house in Assembly Row, close to the Mile End Road, in the parish of Stepney, near the Thames. Some time after James's death, she moved to High Street, Clapham, on the south side of the river.

Note: Although in private she may have called her husband James, she always referred to him in her letters and writings as Mr Cook.

To the Reader

During the long journey of my widowhood, I have been much consoled by my family and our friends, who came to my side whenever the Lord chose to test my faith in His mercy, and by my beloved husband's naval associates who brought me news of their further voyages or chose to recall past events.

Whatever degree of consolation each of these friends afforded me, and I know that it was great, many a day remained when I was left to wander down the dark grove of solitude, for such is the destiny of those who are wedded to men of the sea, whose duties so frequently take them away from those who cherish them, and sometimes cost their lives. My thoughts then returned to the travels of my beloved husband, which I decided to share with him in spirit and to recall, for myself and for others, by a tapestry on which were depicted the sundry episodes which I knew of from his letters to me, from his narratives subsequently published, and from the recollections of those who had known him and shared in his trials and the great deeds he achieved.

Many came to admire as I worked. My faithful companion Mistress Gates watched over every stitch approvingly. Others such as Sir Joseph Banks nodded wisely, and were led to expatiate yet further on the events of thirty years back. Much as an artist will record great deeds or celebrate legends by means of painted canvasses or sculptured marble, so I sought to show the life of a man whom so many praised and I so deeply loved.

As my thoughts followed his voyages, like seabirds following a ship across the wide seas, I dreamed of what it might have been like, had I been by his side, what tasks I might have allotted myself to assist him and ease his work. These dreams I kept a secret lest others smiled at my fancies or silently harboured thoughts of disapproval. Such a voyage, I knew, could never be, not least because of the beloved children the Lord had entrusted into my care, but also because my presence on a ship of our King's Navy would have been against all the ordinances that govern the fleet, and improper for any lady. Sailors indeed are said to fear such a presence on board a vessel for, so they believe, bad luck would ensue.

Others are less filled with the superstitions of the sea, and my Mr Cook had told me of one such woman, who had sailed with the French captain, Louis Bougainville, to minister to the expedition's botanist, whether driven to such a course by a sense of duty or one of love, and had in time completed a circumnavigation of the globe, earning, so it is said, the strictures of some but also the admiration of many for her dutiful perseverance and worthy devotion. So, on some days when pain or loneliness assaulted me and I sat by some window watching the white and grey clouds scurrying past, as though on some errand of great urgency, the fancy took me to toy with thoughts of what I might have done had Fate led me onto those heaving decks.

On many an occasion, Mr Cook had spoken of his work, and shown me how to record bearings and readings, and set them upon a sheet of paper so that, under the ministrations of his quill, a shoreline was drawn and a coastline stretched across, with its indentations and headlands, so I knew that I would have been able to assist him in this work. But he had with him other officers, astronomers and suchlike men of knowledge eager to proffer their help, and no need of a woman's small skill. So my thoughts wandered on to more wifely duties, not solely caring for him and his quarters, exiguous indeed as I well knew, but helping to cope with the difficulties that arose out of the shortage of victuals, which grew so serious as the weeks went past, and the necessity to accommodate the daily fare to the needs of the men by using whatever supplies still remained, or had been brought into the ship through multiple and unexpected circumstances.

And so, slowly but in secret lest, as I have said, mockery or condemnation ensued, I wrote down the thoughts that wandered into my sorrowing mind, brightening the sadness of my days, and from time to time took my writings out of their place of concealment to polish them or add to them, as though I were adding a new stitch to my embroidery.

Should someone discover them, in some later years, and wonder what thoughts lay behind them, let them bear in mind that they consoled me on lonely days. With them, I fled from the gloom of London and the fogs of the river towards realms I could share with my beloved Mr Cook.

Stewed Albatross

It was upon the occasion of a visit from Sir Joseph
Banks, accompanied by Lady Banks, that the
matter of eating the albatross bird arose. Sir Joseph
mentioned that the poet Samuel Coleridge was
earning great praise through a work he had
published, the 'Rime of the Ancient Mariner',
wherein were described great misfortunes that had
befallen some seafaring men through the killing of
an albatross. It was a tale he had read in an
account of a voyage from England to Formosa

undertaken by the privateer George Shelvocke.

Sir Joseph declared that it was a superstition among seamen whose lives are always at the mercy of the ocean, that the death of an albatross would cause much ill-luck among those who were responsible for it, but that it could be dismissed as mere fable. He himself had shared a meal, in which everyone heartily partook and much relished, of an albatross which had been shot two days previous, and no untoward event had resulted. The natives of New Zealand, he had remarked when visiting that country, commonly ate of the albatross, as they did of other seabirds, hunting for them by means of a hook and cord, and no misfortune befell them in consequence.

Lady Banks expressed wonder that such a large bird, which from what she had been told, spent most of its life flying through salty air and feeding upon fish, might be found palatable and even commendable, whereupon Sir Joseph explained how it had been cooked. I decided that I would record this, although such fare would be uncommon indeed in England.

Remove most carefully the feathers, and skin the bird. Leave the carcass over night to soak in salt water, till morn, then parboil it and throw away the water. Then cut up and stew well with a little water, and when sufficiently tender serve up with a savoury sauce.

A prune sauce does well as an accompaniment, as is commonly served with land fowl, but other savoury sauces can be served, with ground ginger or other spices that may be at hand, and a little sugar. When bread, or the sailors' biscuit, is available, it forms a pleasant accompaniment to the meal.

Other Birds of Sea or Land

Many are the navigators who tell of a nourishing repast they enjoyed when sailing close to land having caught some birds or purchased them from native people, or when at sea set lines the seabirds swooped to catch. Thus the French captain La Pérouse has told of being near the Strait of Magellan where were killed and cooked some albatrosses and petrels as well. Skinned with care and cooked, he served them with a piquant sauce and found them to be almost as palatable as the scoter ducks the French eat at Lententime and on Fridays, though they do say that it is tough and only moderately pleasing, but as is known, food taken at that time is meant to be part of a penance for a man's sins.

Lieutenant Peter Puget, who sailed not long ago with Captain Vancouver on a voyage to the northern seas, said that his men, being in need of nourishment, were not averse to eating crows, although some have said it is a salty meat that is not easy to chew even though it be well stewed. Curlews, however, Captain Vancouver and his officers have said, made an excellent repast, more so than the sea eagles they came upon but found to be a coarse meat. Captain La Pérouse told people in New South Wales that his men had eaten curlews and other seabirds they prepared in a salmi, but these were exceedingly thin and tasted and smelled greatly of fish, yet they found them palatable enough, lacking other more appealing fare. Thus, as is often found on such lengthy voyages, sailors will enjoy any food, even though when on land they would turn away from it with great distaste.

Beer, Lemon Juice and Other Anti-scorbutic Beverages

Many were the occasions where Mr Cook spake of the frightful sickness that is scurvy and the sufferings it inflicted on the unfortunate seamen, whose gums became painful and swollen, whose skin became marked as from a pox with evil patches, the blood seemingly seeping through it, and whose limbs became twisted, who gave out a stench that none but other sick sailors could stand, until death came to offer them a release and, as they had had time to repent of any sins committed, opened for them the doors to a happier state. Mr Cook did not concur with those physicians who believed that these ills were caused by evil humours poisoning the blood or the foul air that fills the ship below decks as it does the cells of prisoners in their dungeons and the evil rooms at Bethlehem Hospital, that which they now call Bedlam, where lunatics are immured.

He would ask, often striking his fist upon the table, did not the sailors spend most of their time by far out on deck or aloft in the rigging among wild breezes and fierce gales? And if some physicians sought the source of this plague in the saltiness of the air when a ship was out at sea, how could it so easily attack men in their prisons where no salt air could enter? As many now do, he sought the cause of the scurvy in what the men had to drink or eat.

Water kept in casks and stowed in the holds did become corrupted not long after the ship lost sight of land, giving birth to water-weevils and suchlike creatures. A good shipmaster should seek to keep the water pure, through such as vinegar and molasses being added, or by allowing the men a drink of beer, the which as well I know from my youth in my mother's alehouse, men will readily drink and enjoy, gaining boisterousness therefrom. And beer has properties that kill off the evil humours that spread through the blood. Yet no ship is large enough for all the casks of ale that would be needed for a long voyage and, as he added with a smile, no drayman would ever call to refill the cellar once it had been emptied.

The molasses, which come from sugar, being a syrup, is used by the people of the East Indies to make a drink they call arrack, Sir Joseph Banks reported. They add some rice and the juice of cocoanuts, this giving the beverage its particular flavour which they much prize.

Sir Joseph had been greatly concerned about such matters. He had consulted the eminent John Fothergill, a man of wide botanical knowledge, celebrated for his professional skill and his benevolence, and Nathaniel Hulme, a surgeon of great repute in the Navy, noted for his observations on the scurvy. These two gentlemen advocated the use of lemon juice to counter that evil, and sent Sir Joseph casks containing lemon juice, orange juice, brandy and molasses. I turned my mind to what I would have done to assist in the making of such anti-scorbutic beverages, guided by their advice, had I been on Mr Cook's vessel.

The Brewing of Beer

To a large hogshead of water, be it fresh or but lightly corrupted, add wheat already fermented with a little ale yeast, then two gallons of molasses.

Add to this a little Strasburgh turpentine, which is the juice from the silver fir they grow in Europe, to control the evil that may have corrupted the water.

Yet, sadly, this is but an inferior mixture, and beer, whether taken on at the port of departure or made on board, will rarely keep for more than two weeks. Wine, if it can be got, retains its properties far longer and even if it fails it can be of value as vinegar can.

Beer as traditionally brewed, which in my mother's alehouse was oft sold to those who came there for rest after a day of harsh toil and to partake of same with their friends, was made in accordance with what was, as someone told me, a recipe much favoured in nearby counties such as Norfolk. I note it here to show how well good ale is made on land and how difficult it would be for mariners to repeat such a process when in a distant country.

Take 5 bushels of malt and the same of hops.

Fill the copper quite full and when it boils take away the fire, whereupon wet the malt with 8 pailfuls of water of which just over 3 are taken hot from the copper and just over 4 taken cold from the tub which stands filled with water ready nearby. Then add the rest of the hot water from the copper.

Set the mash and stir it well, covering the tub with sacks. Mark the time when the mash has set and let it stand four hours.

Fill the copper quite full as before and when that water is hot steep in the hops with a sufficiency of hot water to wet them thoroughly. Leave them so till you draw off the first wort.

When the second copper boils, then cover the fire to keep the water hot but not boiling over. Whilst the copper is boiling for the second mash, add thereto one pailful of cold water to make amends for what was taken out to steep the hops.

Note well when the first mash has stood for its four hours, whereupon begin to draw off, returning the wort gently to the top of the mash till the liquor runs clear, then throw water upon it and continue thus till the wort begins to run slow.

Take the fire down and throw the whole copperful of hot water upon the mash tub, stirring it well and covering it once again. Then put the first wort with the hops into the copper and make up the fire.

Run the first wort from the copper through the sieve into the copper.

Put the hops into the copper once again and draw off the second wort, putting it into the copper, raise the fire and watch when it begins to boil. Let it do so for half an hour as before, then take the fire down completely.

Carry out the dregs and clean the mash tub, then put the second wort from the copper into it, running it through a sieve.

As soon as you can, set out two or three pailfuls of the first wort abroad in the meadow to cool faster so that you can begin the working. By this means you secure a second fermentation and let the liquor in the cooler be near enough cold before you add it to the working wort.

Then draw the second wort from the mash tub, and when cool enough return it to the mash tub and set it to work.

If in summer, when the warmth would slow the cooling, take the tub down into the beer cellar.

With the whole quantity, this can make in all 87 gallons of good beer.

Spruce Beer

Mr Cook on his sad last voyage did brew a beer made with the twigs and leaves of the spruce tree, that fir tree some call the Prussian tree. This he did while sailing off the coast of the north-west of America, wisely using the resources that God had placed near at hand. A learned person, John Treslove his name, had advised the Admiralty of this, confirming what some colonists had written, that a Frenchman Jacques Cartier, sailing to that continent many years ago, had been shown the beneficial uses of spruce by the local natives, thus curing his crew who were sickening from the scurvy. I have discovered that there are several ways of preparing spruce beer and making it most palatable to sailors.

Take 1 pound of light dry malt extract
6 pounds of light malt syrup
3 cups of crystal malt
1 cup of wheat
2 ounces of hops

2 to 3 cups of blue spruce twigs
1 cup of spruce green needles, lightly boiled

Let the hops be boiled for one hour, the spruce twigs crushed then boiled for one half of an hour. Mix well in water that has been boiling but a moment before, then allow to cool and to settle. Such impurities as may appear on the surface are to be removed, the beverage carefully poured out when it has fermented, and further impurities having fallen to the bottom of the cauldron will thus be left behind.

The men might not each one find this palatable, being bitter, but will be cheered by the dark colour of the beverage, thinking of the stout they have drunk in the alehouses. Whether as sundry persons have said, this resembles the strong beer they call 'stingo' in the county of Yorkshire, which some praise as exceedingly palatable as well as promoting good health, I cannot tell.

The Addition of Lemon Juice

Dr Nathaniel Hulme did urge Sir Joseph Banks to make use of the juice of lemons, which was often pressed and then boiled whole to ensure that it remained uncorrupted in the casks, and to obtain further supplies whenever the ship called at any place abroad where such could be obtained. This is a wise move by any mariner, though Mr Cook himself did place greater score on malt and fresh vegetables when these could be obtained. Doctor Lind has advised similarly in his Treatise on the Scurvy.

Orange Juice with Brandy

Dr Hulme also sent some orange juice to which brandy had been added for its greater preservation, yet it did not keep well, some of it possibly having leaked out and the sea air entered to corrupt it, for it was covered with the white mould they call 'mother'. It was not damaged to the taste, but soon when placed in bottles it became sour and unpleasant. It was resolved, Sir Joseph said, to evaporate it to a strong essence and bottle it to use later. It is indeed a hard task on such long voyages to ensure that food and beverages do keep.

'Tis said that on the voyage of the much-lamented French captain La Pérouse, who has disappeared in the southern ocean, candied lemons and the like were shipped, as such though costly to buy do keep for lengthy periods and are most palatable as well as beneficial to the health.

Local Beverages

The wise mariner will seek what he can use to make a healthy beverage in the distant countries where fate leads him. Thus he will seek out the spruce fir in the northern countries, but in the islands far away in the southern ocean, known as New Zealand, Mr Cook was told of a tree they called the tea-tree which the native people use; it can be cooked to make a health-giving food, and possesses a juice that flows abundantly from which a beverage can be made, likened by some to a beer but by others to a tea, tolerably good though sweet. In later years, men who sailed to the south of these islands to hunt the seal and suchlike made use of the tea-tree for a tolerable good beverage not unlike that made from the leaves of the shrubs of India, and as was reported not many years ago, some by mixing it with spruce did make a beer-like beverage, all these being very wholesome for men in such circumstances.

In some islands of the same ocean is made a drink more like spirits than beer, which they called a kava or ava, from a shrub some call the pepper plant. They report that it is made by young girls or boys who, having rinsed their mouths with seawater, chew the leaves which they then place in a bowl, then pour over them water or the juice of fruits, stirring it well. It is left to ferment, after which the dregs and other sediment are removed with great care, a liquid with a greenish hue or on other occasions the colour of pale coffee being produced and oft drunk with great ceremonials.

These same islands are the home of a tree on which the large nuts they call cocoa do grow, in the centre of which an abundant juice is found. Sir Joseph Banks reported that the islanders partake readily of this, dipping every morsel of fish into it and drinking large sups of it, so that a man may use one half-pint of it at a meal. From the kernel of these cocoanuts, once fermented, they make a sauce, the taste of which is very strong and which he found 'abominable nauseous'. However, a very little use of it reconciled him entirely with it so that, he quoth, 'I should almost prefer it to our own sauces with fish.' The odour could be improved, though a little, by the addition of some sweet flowers or a scented wood some call the 'sandal wood', and thereafter use as an oil to anoint their skin and their hair.

Biscuits

Of considerable importance to seamen is the ship's biscuit, which some are known to describe as hard tack, a term which is commonly used for a length of lead or for a broad-headed nail, yet this hard consistency is of the utmost value in preserving it for lengthy periods such as are imposed by the necessities of navigation.

To ensure this preservation, care is taken in the storing thereof, before it is placed in cases or sacks as well as when it is stored on board ship. A special storing space is often set aside for biscuits, thus to ensure that they remain dry and do not lose their hardness, yet this is difficult to ensure during all the travails of storms and navigation through differing climes, and the biscuit can suffer from the depredations of the vermin that appear within it. Sir Joseph Banks expatiated at some length on the condition of the hard tack in the *Endeavour*, stating that as they sailed to the island of Otaheite the biscuit was so full of vermin that, notwithstanding all his care, he sometimes had as many as twenty in his mouth, every one of them tasting as hot as mustard. On a further occasion, he told us that that 'hundreds, nay thousands' were shaken out of a single biscuit, though I confess that on this occasion I did suspect his words to carry with them some little exaggeration.

A remedy, the which he outlined as carried out by those in the Great Cabin, was to bake the biscuit anew in a moderate oven, whereby the vermin did all walk off. But such a remedy could not be allowed to the ordinary seamen who sought other ways, such as dipping the hard tack, or broken pieces thereof if struck with a hammer, into a small vat of seawater, which caused the vermin to swim to the surface, there to be scooped off and thrown overboard. A savant of great renown, with a great curiosity for all things scientific, he set before us a list of the vermin that so infested the biscuit, namely some he called Tenebrios, one named Ptinus and others Phalangium.

Notwithstanding the unpleasant effects of dampness seeping into the tack and enabling the vermin to generate themselves, the biscuits are much prized as a victual for mariners on long voyages, as also by soldiers on lengthy campaigns through territories where food is scarce, as we have seen in the recent wars. Indeed, Count Rumford, who not many years back wrote a valued tome on food, observed that 'hard and stale bread renders mastication necessary, and mastication seems powerfully to assist in promoting digestion. It likewise prolongs the duration of the enjoyment of eating, a matter of very great importance indeed.'

Take flour, water and salt as follows: 2 cups of flour, add 1 cup of water, and season with 4 to 6 pinches of salt. It is thought that less salt will be

*required for ship's biscuits, but more for soldiers'
tack. Mix all together and knead well until a dough
has formed of a strong consistency.*

*Roll to a thickness of 1 inch, cut into the shape
of a square or a rectangle as is desired, then bake
until brown.*

*Allow the biscuit to cool, but soon test its
hardness, and unless it has become a satisfactory
hard tack return to the oven, having let its heat
cool a little. Often a cook must bake the biscuit yet
again for greater hardness.*

*As the circumstances permit, consume the
biscuit after you have soaked it in a soup or light
broth, whether of fish or meat. If broken up into
pieces, it may be placed in the broth, then well
stirred and let to lie for a little while, to make a
meal of greater consistency.*

Dog Stewed and in Broth

In London, dogs are much prized, some tended like children, others more hardy companions fed or allowed to seek what food may remain in streets and, as I well knew, allowed to wander into alehouses to consume scraps dropped by revellers. In distant countries, however, they themselves are turned into food, faithful and trusting companions though they may have been. Sailors to such places often have purchased dogs or been given some by the natives they encounter, and a great blessing they can prove as happened to Mr Cook when sickness struck him down in cold climes while sailing in the ship *Resolution* near the island they call Easter. Mr Reinhold Forster ordered a dog which he had obtained in the island of Otaheite to be killed and cut into quarters, which were served to Mr Cook during several days. Thus was his life preserved.

Sir Joseph Banks reports on the practice the islanders of Otaheite adopted to cook their dogs, 'dressing him up in the same manner as we would do a pig, singeing him over the fire that was lit to roast him and scraping him clean with a shell. He then opened him with the same instrument and taking out his entrails sent them to the sea where they were most carefully washed and then put into cocoanut shells with what blood he had found in him. Stones were then laid out and the dog well covered with leaves laid upon them. In about two hours he was dressed, and in another quarter of an hour completely eat.' A most excellent dish, said Sir Joseph, for those who were not much prejudiced against such species of food. He further said that a South Sea dog was next to English lamb, and that the taste was due to their living entirely on vegetables.

The skin is then made into cloaks and much valued in such islands as New Zealand, as the French can testify who called there at the same time as Mr Cook and were given a cloak by a local chief in exchange for a shirt, a singlet and trousers of red cloth, this colour being much prized. Another French mariner, Monsieur Louis Bougainville, while sailing through the Strait of Magellan was given dogs by the natives, which later on their voyage, being greatly in want of fresh food, they killed and cooked, judging it as did Sir Joseph to be most palatable.

Should circumstances be such that sailors are forced to eat a dog, a good dish may be prepared in the following fashion:

Kill a medium-size dog, then burn off the fur over a hot fire. Carefully remove the skin while still warm and set aside.

Cut the meat into cubes of one inch, then

marinade for 2 hours in a mixture of vinegar, pepper and saltwater.

Fry the meat in oil over an open fire, then add onions or fruit as may be at hand such as orange or pineapple.

Take from the fire and pour in boiling water with tomato sauce, green pepper and if such be available a piquant sauce.

Cover and allow to simmer over warm coals until the meat is tender. Blend in some flavouring such as liver and let it cook for an additional 5 to 7 minutes.

To Stew:

Cut your dog meat into cubes or small slices, put into a stewpot.

Add a little wine such as claret and a little vinegar, a sprig or two of rosemary, some cloves, a little sugar and some grated bread or pieces of hard biscuit.

Allow to stew very gently for 2 hours, then stir in

a grating of nutmegs and let stew for 15 minutes.

Then serve, well garnished with sliced oranges or other fruit.

From this can be drawn a most nourishing broth if someone is sick and unable to digest more solid food, as was the case with Mr Cook.

Breadfruit and Suchlike

As he sails to distant places, the mariner will encounter fruit of sundry varieties which may be nourishing and palatable. Of these, one is the breadfruit which Captain Bligh has struggled to bring from the southern ocean to the islands of the Caribbean Sea, greatly suffering in this endeavour. The breadfruit in recent times is found in Covent Garden, though many are wary of this alien fruit. Yet it holds a pleasing white pulp that can be baked into biscuit or bread and made into a sweet pudding.

Roasted Breadfruit

Take 1 breadfruit which roast whole over a fire. They do say that if charcoal be used the taste will be more flavoursome. Turn it well to ensure all is lightly charred. Steam will form that escapes from the stem end, and when that is seen remove the breadfruit from the fire. Cut a circle at the stem end and scoop out the heart, which discard. Scoop out the meat or cut off the outer skin that is now charred. Cut the meat into slices and serve.

Other fruit that are found are the banana, which if yellow but not green can be eaten raw, but also fried or served in fritters or with a pudding. The cocoanut is abundant on the islands of the ocean and is much used by the peoples there. Sir Joseph Banks also spoke of other fruit and plants which he assured us would one day be much valued by Englishmen and also found on stalls in Covent Garden.

Fish, Fresh and Potted

Those who have never ventured on the sea are heard to say that sailors can never feel hungry because fish is so plentiful, but they do not know that a ship travels too fast through waves and storms for a line or a net to be lowered and fish caught therein. Far out at sea dwell large fish that are not easily caught, although when they are their flesh is greatly welcome.

Captain Philip Carteret, who sailed around the world in his ship *Swallow* a little before Mr Cook, has reported that crossing the southern ocean one of his sailors struck with a harpoon a fish called a yellowtail, from the colour of his tail, which he ordered to be made into broth for his sick people, an agreeable event he has said for they had been a long time without fish. Not long after this fortunate catch three sharks were seen swimming about the vessel, whereupon with hooks which they baited with pieces of salt meat the sailors caught all three, which they divided equally between the officers and men. Although a very strong meat, they found it most agreeable, it being fresh food which they sadly had lacked for many days.

In more recent years, Captain Vancouver spoke of a feast offered by the people of Otaheite, at which were served a large tunny fish and a porpoise 'cut up in small pieces entrails and all and placed into a large trough with a mixture of water, blood and fish oil, and the whole stewed by throwing stones into it', this method of cooking being common among these people who know nothing of iron and therefore have no stew pots.

I thought many times about how I might have cooked fish had some been caught during a voyage, when all the men were in dire need of sustenance but spices and condiment were scarce. Stewing seemed to be the best means since so much of the fish can be used and being well stirred with whatever flavourings one may have would make a nourishing meal. Frying is more wasteful because slices of the fish are cut away and usually so much is thrown aside, yet even these parts, bones and fins, can be dropped into a stew. What I would have greatly wished to do was to serve up fish in pastry which is exceedingly palatable or bring aboard potted fish hoping it could be preserved for some days before becoming too foul to eat.

Fish in Pastry

Take one whole fish weighing not less than 1 pound, gut and bone it but leave the head and the tail. Wash it well, then dry it (some use paper, others some cloth).

Season it inside with salt, pepper, mace and ginger, and insert slivers of butter, about 1½ ounces in all.

Having prepared 1 pound of shortcrust or puff pastry, roll this into the shape of a large oval, 2 inches at each end longer than the fish, making sure that it will be wide enough to fold over the fish and have left 1 or 2 inches to seal it.

Transfer most carefully the fish onto the pastry, its belly towards you. Then fold the pastry over and trim the excess, adjusting the head and tail to display the shape of the fish. Seal with water and crimp the edge. With the back of a small spoon, design scales and fins upon the pastry, and with a raisin give him an eye.

Beat the white of an egg and a good spoonful of milk then drop this upon the pastry, lightly as a rain that drizzles down. Do not brush it on lest you destroy the design of the scales but use a brush to ensure that it is but lightly sprinkled.

Bake it well in a good heat for 10 minutes until it begins to colour, then for 20 minutes in a lesser heat. If the fish is short and thick then more minutes may be required.

Set it to cool a little, then serve within a line of sliced lemons or suchlike.

Potted Fish

Salmon is best if such is available. A friend gave me a recipe popular in the northern counties near the town of Newcastle upon Tyne.

Take 4 pieces of salmon cut into steaks each one weighing 6 or so ounces.

Wipe the salmon and season well with a quarter ounce of ground mace, a quarter ounce of ground cloves and a little pepper.

Place in a dish and dot with a little unsalted butter.

Cover and bake for 30 or 40 minutes, occasionally basting the steaks with the liquid.

Lift out the salmon steaks and allow them to drain then to cool a little, then remove all skin and bones and flake the flesh finely.

Place in 4 to 6 ramekin dishes and press down well.

Spoon melted butter over the fish to seal, then leave to set.

Keep in as cold a place as you can find, then serve with buttered crusty bread or toasted bread.

Otter Meat

Whether this be a fish or a land animal that spends much of its life in the sea, a subject of some disputations among learned men, it provides good nourishment and a palatable meat, so that it is much hunted, some people even using a dog they train for the purpose, which some call the otter-dog, but most catching them out at sea. They are covered with a fur, much prized in cold regions, which is removed whole before the meat is cooked. Captain Vancouver has spoken of the Kodiak people in northern lands who dry the furs and trade them, and consider the meat a great delicacy. They scrape the blubber or fat from the carcass, eating it with the greatest relish in its raw state. The rest of the animal is then boiled, and wild vegetables procured in and about the woods are added to the stew to afford a most excellent repast. Any mariners venturing into the seas thereabouts would do well to seek the otter for their sustenance.

Jellyfish

Mariners call these creatures 'blubber'. Few favour the eating thereof, but the lack of victuals turns many things into a food that can relieve hunger. Some of the people in the islands of the southern ocean do eat regularly of them, for as Sir Joseph Banks has stated, 'custom will make almost any meat palatable', and they are favoured by the women there, although he added that 'After they had eat it I confess I was not extremely fond of their company'. So I would not prepare such a dish in London, but in my mind I have thought that circumstances might have forced me to do so if fate had led me to accompany Mr Cook on his travels.

Some of these creatures are of an exceedingly tough nature, but are prepared by suffering them to stink. Best are those that are of a larger size, as these can most easily be cut into strips or shredded.

Take about ½ pound of dried jellyfish which rinse well and shred

½ small spoonful of salt
1 spoonful of vinegar
2 small spoonfuls of piquant sauce such as soy
2 small spoonfuls of sugar
3 spoonfuls of sesame oil
A small number of sesame seeds which then toast

Rinse the jellyfish in cold water and drain. Fill a pan with boiling water in which place the jellyfish and let it stand in this for about 15 minutes, which should make it tender. Drain and again soak several times in cold water, then drain carefully and put aside. Mix the soy sauce, the sesame oil and sugar, stir into a smooth sauce and into this toss the jellyfish. Stir and let stand for some 30 minutes. Sprinkle over this the sesame seeds and serve.

The jellyfish can also be cooked with turnips, which must be peeled and shredded, then sprinkled with salt, boiled very lightly then let stand for one hour. Drain well and place these in a serving bowl with the jellyfish previously dried and then cut into very thin slices of 1 to 1½ inches in length. Add a little of the vinegar. Some recommend it be then boiled lightly, cooled, then over this should be sprinkled some soy sauce, a good spoonful of sesame oil and one of sugar and what is left of the vinegar. Stir and toss, then place over this a sprig or more of parsley to decorate.

Goat, Roast and Stewed

Mr Cook stood on our doorstep one day on his return from the voyage of the ship *Endeavour*, holding a goat on a rope much like a servant exercising his master's dog. 'I have brought this goat home for us to care for,' he said. 'She has twice sailed round the world and has been a great companion. Now she may spend the remainder of her days in peaceful retirement.' And indeed she remained with me and the children happy in our small backyard in Mile End Road. And many were those who came to see her, as did Sir Joseph Banks and even Lord Sandwich who stood, as he said, hat in hand 'To pay his respects'.

Goats are indeed a valued companion for mariners on long voyages, for unlike the cattle and the poultry they take with them on deck the goat can survive on very little nourishment: some straw if any be left, any scraps of greens of any kind and even scraps of clothing and frayed rope. In return they furnish the captain and officers with a milk that is most nutritious, even more beneficial than cow's milk so some assure me. In return they receive much gratitude and affection and it is reported that when a dire insufficiency of victuals forced Monsieur Bougainville to sacrifice his goat there was great sorrow on his ship and the cook wept as he prepared his knife for this sad occasion.

Goat meat and goat stew are much prized. 'Tis said that at the funerary feast of King Midas in ancient times was served a dish of marinated and barbecued goat meat seasoned with lentils with a beer made of thyme, honey and grapes with added barley malt and saffron. More palatable of course is the flesh of the young goat, the which can be served roasted, but older goats such as those that would sail on long voyages are best stewed, their meat being less easy to masticate than lamb or mutton which some say it resembles.

Roast Goat Meat

Take 3½ pounds of goat with the bones.
Peel and quarter 4 medium potatoes and the same with 3 onions but large.
Chop finely some parsley to make 4 small spoonfuls.

Place the potatoes and the onions in a large pot to which add the garlic and sprinkle thereon the parsley. Add water enough to cover and let cook over a medium flame for half an hour.

Then place the meat in a deep baking dish and sprinkle over a small spoonful of salt and one of pepper and rosemary. Cover the meat with the vegetables and 2 cups of the liquid wherein they were boiled. Bake in medium heat for 2 hours, basting occasionally with the fluids.

To serve, remove the meat and vegetables from the liquids that remain. These latter can at some later time be used in a broth.

Stewed Goat

For this dish, cut 2¼ pounds of goat meat into cubes or small pieces.
Slice 2 large onions but thickly.
Prepare also 3 whole cloves, 1 small spoonful of flour and 2 of butter.
Boil some rice for later serving.

In a heavy pan melt the butter and then add the onions until just translucent. Whereupon add the meat, increase the heat so that it may brown speedily. Then add the cloves and some piquant sauce, with a little salt and pepper. Some who favour this taste may add up to 2 cloves of garlic coarsely chopped.

Pour sufficient water thereon to cover and bring to the boil and when this is done simply simmer for some 2 hours, skimming at times.

One quarter of an hour before the end of the cooking, pour enough of the liquid to make a paste with the flour. A flavouring of spice such as a chilli may be added, and some also pour over it a little of the piquant sauce. Stir this paste into the stew and continue cooking, stirring well, until it thickens.

Ready the boiled rice, over which the stew will be served, all this while hot.

Gruel

Although persons of quality or of some substance look down upon it, gruel can be a most appealing and nourishing dish with the addition of small quantities of such flavourings as may be available. For mariners it is of special value as it is simple to prepare and can contain leftovers of cereals which conditions in the hold and the depredation of rodents and vermin may have tarnished, and thereby sailors who are suffering through an insufficiency of food may be restored to health.

When it has been made the gruel will keep, to be served cold, if more has been made than is first required.

Water Gruel

Take 1 pint of water and 1 large spoonful of oatmeal.

Stir well together and begin to boil it for 2 to 4 minutes, stirring often.

Ensure that it will not boil over. Then strain it through a sieve. If water is already salted, as is seawater, it will do well, but if not, salt it now a little.

Add 1 half ounce of butter or less, which stir until all melted. Thus it will be fine and smooth.

Some persons who do not like it plain may add some raisins and mace, or even sack, that which they call Spanish sherry, but mariners may have little of such enhancements. It is notwithstanding most nourishing and palatable.

Barley Gruel

Take 1 pint of water and 2 ounces of barley, pearl barley being best.

Stir into a smooth paste, which pour into a pan containing 1 pint of boiling water or milk. Place this on the fire for 10 minutes while stirring well, then pour into a basin.

Add a pinch of salt unless the water has been earlier salted, and a little sugar. Some favour the addition of a little butter if such be available.

Add just a little white wine and then serve.

The dish they call frumenty is made with hulled wheat in the place of barley. Sugar but also cinnamon can flavour it, and enriching the mixture with the yolk of an egg and cream gives a special dish many favour at Yuletide.

Count Rumford greatly praised barley, a most nutritional food which could make an excellent soup if cooked as a gruel but better still if potatoes and peas were added. The cook will use vinegar and salt, but no sugar for such a dish. He recommended that it be served to the poor who greatly suffered from hunger in times of poor crops or other troubles.

Rats in Stew

A plague in all vessels bound for distant ports are the rats which infest the holds, filled as these are with stores, ropes, spare canvas and suchlike equipment so that they can hide and breed in utter safety. Sailors who catch them throw them into the sea, but a shortage of victuals may force them to seek them as nourishment. Thus it happened on the voyage of Monsieur Bougainville when, having sailed across the southern ocean and being in dire need of fresh meat and tasty broth, two of his gentlemen caught a rat which they took to the cook to prepare and ate with great relish. This they did again but were seen by the men who went below decks to hunt, whereupon the gentlemen expressed concern that this source of food which they now prized so highly might be no more, although being Frenchmen they favoured a daintier cuisine. For their good fortune, their ship not long thereafter came to some land where refreshments could be got.

Stewed Rats

First catch your rat, then singe over a flame to rid the skin of any furry cover.

Remove the tips of the paws to rid the animal of its claws, wash the body in water and gut, setting the entrails aside.

Stamp the rat in a stone mortar till the bones are well broken and crushed as you might when preparing cock ale and if you see them throw away the teeth.

Place in a goodly pint of boiling water, stir and

add such flavourings as you may have, such as a little grated nutmeg, pepper black and a little vinegar.

Wash well the entrails which then cut very finely and crush, all this in saltwater to give flavour, then add to the mix.

When the boiling has proceeded for 5 minutes, no more, add a quarter pint of saltwater, lower well the fire to stew all the ingredients, not forgetting the entrails.

Stir gently and cover the pot well, leaving it to simmer over the low fire for 1 hour or less.

Add broken tack or crumbed stale bread if any be left, stir in gently, then serve.

Greater numbers of rats than one will make a more serviceable stew.

Sauerkraut or Pickled Cabbage

There has been much talk of this dish in recent times and one Dr Trotter not long since has written that sauerkraut did possess great value against the scurvy. The Navy itself has long added sauerkraut to the supplies it gives to ships leaving for distant voyages. Captains Carteret and Wallis fed their men this pickled cabbage, whether it be the yellow cabbage or the red, and Mr Cook likewise. Sir Joseph Banks, although not partial to this dish which some call 'a stinking preparation of cabbage', being cut in the month of November, then fermented with salt and vinegar after which it is pressed, gave me his recipe. I did think that if Fate had led me onto the ship I would have been able to make similar preparations with cabbages we would have purchased ashore, there being vinegar aplenty on board and salt abundant in the seawater around.

Take a strong iron bound cask, take out the head and when the whole is well cleaned cover the bottom with salt. Then take the cabbage and stripping off the outside leaves, take the rest leaf by leaf till you come to the heart which cut into 4. These leaves and heart then lay upon the salt about 2 or 3 inches thick and sprinkle more salt pretty thick over them. Do the same until the cask is full, then lay on the head of the cask with a weight which in 5 or 6 days will have pressed the cabbage into a much smaller compass. Then fill the cask with more cabbage as above directed and close it up. It is best to gather the cabbage after the sun is well risen, so that no dew lies upon it, and note that halves of cabbage will keep longer than the single leaves.

This dish, said Sir Joseph, they had eaten every day since leaving Cape Horn and found as good to their palates and as pleasing to the eye as if it was bought fresh at Covent Garden market.

Turtle Soup

Many seamen encounter diverse kinds of turtles on the islands of the Atlantic Ocean and of the great southern ocean, and they are much praised by them, being most flavoursome and nourishing, the best among them being the green turtle which they report has a taste that reminds them of the best veal. Being sluggish in movement and much given to stay on land, they are easy to catch and when upturned cannot escape.

Captain Vancouver has recently reported that

upon leaving the coast of California he easily procured as many turtles as he could dispense with, but later was glad to catch bonitos, albacores and other fish, which made good amends for the deficiency of turtles, now almost consumed and of which they had had so many that he believed most of his men had by then become tired of them. Sir Joseph Banks found such large turtles among a great reef that lies off the coast of New Holland that a single one sufficed to feed all the company.

Take 1 to 1½ pounds of turtle meat
One large onion, which chop coarsely
Two ribs of celery, which chop coarsely
Some beef stock or the like
A little tomato, crushed or in sauce

Place these ingredients into a 4-quart pot and heat until boiling; then lower to a simmer and cook thus for one hour.

Remove the meat which cut into pieces no larger than one half inch, and return to the pot.

Then add 2 bay leaves, 2 small spoonfuls of mace

and 1 or 1½ spoonfuls of lemon juice; add a small cup of wine, then let simmer further for 1 hour.

Then add 2 egg whites previously cooked hard and chopped, and a little cup of parsley also chopped.

Simmer on for 2 or 3 minutes, stir most gently and 'twill be ready.

Turtle Soup as in the Caribbean islands

This I am told is a meal which the people of these islands greatly favour.

Take 3 lbs of turtle meat well cleaned.

Take 1 large cup of vegetable oil, which place in a 2-gallon pot, heat well, then add 1 cup of flour and stir well with a whisk.

Add 2 cups of chopped onions, 2 cups of chopped celery and 1 cup of chopped tomatoes and 1 cup of pepper.

Cook this for 3 to 5 minutes, then add the turtle meat with a little diced ham. Stir most carefully and cook for 8 to 10 minutes more, then add 4 quarts of chicken stock, one ladle at a time until all is poured in.

Add 2 bay leaves, a little thyme, mace, nutmeg and such, and sprinkle in a large spoonful of lemon juice.

Simmer for 1½ hours or until the meat is well tender.

Add 3 well boiled eggs chopped and a little salt and pepper.

To Welcome Home a Weary Mariner

It was a great and joyful occasion when news came of the safe return of the voyagers and when not long after their safe landing Mr Cook appeared on our doorstep, bearing gifts from distant lands and greeting the children with great embraces. For many weeks as I learned of his progress towards England and along the Channel, I had planned how best I could welcome him with dishes that would console him for the harsh fare he had endured for such long months, return him to health and help him to celebrate the England that he had left behind to set off on such distant and dangerous travels. No more of the pease soup, the hog's pudding and cabbage, the dry biscuit and bread which had been served to him day after day, and even on numerous occasions had been lacking.

Roast beef and ale are the backbone of England, as Mr Blackburn my stepfather was much given to proclaim as he raised his glass in tribute to the dish my mother so often prepared. But Mr Cook was a Yorkshireman and I always made certain when in turn I prepared a meal for my husband that Yorkshire pudding was served at those first meals after his return. Roast beef would accompany this dish, and I knew which merchant I would send to for the most fresh and most nourishing meat and which cow keeper was the best to supply our milk. There was a gardener in Whitechapel who sold in season the most appetising peaches and plums, of which we could partake during the meal, although bagpuddings and pasties I ever seasoned with raisins.

Yorkshire Pudding

Take a small cup of bacon dripping but half filled
A goodly cup of milk little more than half filled
One egg, which beat well
Half a cup of flour which sift well
A little salt

Combine the egg with the milk and beat until light, then gradually beat in the sifted flour and sprinkle the salt. When smooth, let this stand for 30 minutes or a little less.

Pour in 2 tablespoons of the bacon dripping into a pan which heat in the oven, watch over it lest it begin to smoke, then pour in the batter and bake in the hot oven. Serve as soon as it is done lest it deflate, and pour a little hot beef gravy over it. This will serve 4 people.

Roast Beef

Take a goodly rib of beef of 4 to 5 lbs. It is best if it has a layer of fat as this will give you juice for the basting and keep the meat moist and flavoursome. If while it cooks you dust it with a medium spoonful of mustard powder and some plain flour which you have seasoned with a little salt and pepper, the fat will become pleasantly crusty as it cooks.

In the roasting tin place 2 small halves of a fresh onion to flavour the gravy. Over this place the meat, the tin well in the centre of the oven. Cook well for 20 minutes, then let the fire be less hot and cook the meat for a further 1½ hours, basting well every ½ hour. Cook a little longer if you wish the beef well done.

When cooked to your satisfaction, let the meat rest in a warm place before serving, as it will relax and carve with greater ease. Gravy will seep; pour this over the meat no more than once, then collect to pour over the Yorkshire pudding. Serve the beef with roasted potatoes or some other vegetables if these be in season and a little creamed horseradish.

Fried Celery

The cook would serve most vegetables plain boiled with a little melted butter poured over, but some nowadays favour fried celery for a special dish.

Take 1 or several heads of celery, in all some 12 ounces
5 ounces of plain flour
2 egg yolks
Half a small spoon of nutmeg well grated and the same of salt
4 ounces of white wine
A little clarified butter, being butter which you have melted and filtered or let stand to take away the buttermilk

Mix the flour, the salt and the nutmeg in a bowl, then make a well in the middle in which drop the egg yolks. Add a tablespoon of white wine. Mix, stirring in the flour, then gradually add the remaining wine. Leave this to stand.

Cut the celery into slices some 5 inches in length

which simmer in boiling water until almost tender but not softened. Drain well and pat until dry. Dip each celery piece into the batter to completely coat it, then fry in the clarified butter for about 2 minutes until golden. I like to pour a little melted butter over them before they are served.

Jugged Pigeons

Land fowl was most appealing after the seabirds so often salty and hard that the sailors had eaten on the voyage. In London, chicken was common and not expensive, to form the basis of many a pleasing dish, but pigeons were oft landed from upriver and offered for sale at stalls not distant from our house. Stewing was a means some might use, but cooking the birds in a tall closed pot without gravy added gave us jugged birds which Mr Cook greatly enjoyed.

For this, I sent for 6 pigeons which I would wash and dry well. Then stuffing would be used with great care, having been made earlier from these ingredients.

1 half pound of fresh breadcrumbs
1 half pound of suet, well chopped
A small spoonful of salt, 1 of pepper and 1 of
nutmeg well grated
4 spoonfuls of parsley, chopped
2 ounces of butter, grated
2 egg yolks, hard boiled then mashed

Mix well together and squeeze a little lemon over,
then add one egg beaten. When the stuffing has
been placed in each of the birds, sew the vents with
a needle and thread. Place all in a large jug over
which place pieces of a chopped celery. To seal the
jug, mix flour with water to make a thick dough
that can be moulded around the edge of the lid.
Then place in a deep pan or pail, which fill with
boiling water to cover all, and let boil for 3 hours.

Prepare a beurre manié with 1 ounce of butter
and 1 ounce of flour, which knead well together
with the fingers. Lay the birds onto a dish, well
heated, and pour the juices into a small pan, which
boil, adding small pieces of the beurre manié. Pour
this gravy over the birds and garnish with slices of

*lemon, giving a pleasing appearance to the dish as
well as a pleasing taste.*

Oyster Loaves

These make a most appealing side dish or as a first
dish to serve which the French call an entrée, oysters
being easy to obtain fresh along the river. Oysters
are simple to cook by dipping well in prepared
batter then fried in lard, but served in a lightly
toasted small loaf they will delight the partakers. For
this you will require 4 lightly cooked but small
loaves, of no more than 2 ounces each.

Take 4 ounces of butter, which melt
12 fresh oysters, small are best
A pinch of nutmeg, grated
A pinch of ground mace
A little white wine

*Cut away the top of the loaves and scoop out much
of the middle. Lightly cover the underside of the
tops and the hollows of the rolls with a little of the*

melted butter, and toast until lightly golden, this being done in the oven.

Lightly fry the oysters in what remains of the melted butter for 2 or 3 minutes, tossing this carefully until the edges begin to curl. Then add a little wine and the spices. This done, place 3 oysters in each of the 4 hot loaves, cover them with their tops and serve.

Strawberries as Fritters

When the strawberries are in season and on the stalls of the sellers nearby they can be served as fritters, which are most agreeable to conclude a meal. They should be well dry and 'tis best to leave the stalks on them.

1 pound of large strawberries will suffice, with 6 ounces of flour and 2 ounces of crushed sugar
2 small spoonfuls of nutmeg, grated
2 eggs, which beat well
8 ounces of cream
Some lard

Sift the flour into a bowl, onto which sprinkle the sugar, which is best done with a caster, and the nutmeg. Make a hollow in the centre as a well and therein pour the eggs and the cream. Stir this well until all is mixed, then let stand for an hour or even two. Dip each strawberry into this batter until it be wholly coated, and fry a few at a time in the lard hot enough to puff them but not so hot as it will brown them too quickly. Drain this out and keep well hot, making a pile onto a hot dish, then sprinkle some sugar and serve.

Poor Knights Pudding

Mr Cook was partial to this dish, which is easy to make and oft served in our home. When he was sailing off the land of New Zealand he sighted some islands which made him think of this delicacy, which he now sorely missed, being so far away from home, and so he gave them the name of 'Poor Knights Islands'.

Take 4 thick slices of bread
2 eggs
A small spoonful of sugar, well crushed
A small spoonful of cinnamon, ground
6 or 7 ounces of milk

Beat well the eggs, the milk, the sugar and the cinnamon, all together. Cut the bread into quarters; cutting off the crusts is best. Pour the mixture over the bread, and leave to soak some 3 minutes.

Heat some oil in a pan, ready for frying. Drain the bread and slide carefully into the pan, then fry until golden brown on both sides. Sprinkle over this the sugar and the cinnamon.

Some prefer to use a little sweet white wine instead of the milk. And some may add a little preserve such as strawberry jam to flavour the dish, in that case using it instead of the sugar.

The Hasty Pudding

I was most partial to this dish when a girl and still find it most pleasing. It is good to serve and simple to make.

Take 1 large pint of milk
4 spoonfuls of flour
A little nutmeg grated
5 eggs
A little sugar
A little butter or more if the weather is cold

Mix the flour into the milk, stirring well, then boil into a smooth runny pudding. Sprinkle in the sugar as well to suit your taste, and add the nutmeg. Let it cool and when almost cold, beat the eggs together very well and stir this into the pudding.

Butter your bowl or if you wish several smaller custard cups and pour in your mixture. Tie a cloth over all and place into a pan of boiling water. Let them boil for something more than half an hour. When ready to serve pour over it a little melted butter.

Pumpkin Pie

This simple though most palatable dish was a favourite of my good Mistress Gates. She often persuaded me to offer this pie to Mr Cook and the children or to visitors, whereupon she would in haste go to a stallkeeper she knew who sold the best and the freshest pumpkins, and returned in equal haste talking to no one and never slowing to watch some street argument or other scene that normally would greatly amuse her. Then she entered the house, bearing the pumpkin as in triumph and set to preparing the pie in the kitchen whence all but she would then be banished.

Most partial to this dish was Sir Joseph Banks, for he had met it in the East Indies where it was made with lemon juice and sugar or used as a substitute for turnip 'not to be despised' when flavoured with pepper and salt. It keeps well for several months and thus sailors much appreciated it. Mistress Gates, notwithstanding his praise, kept to her own recipe which none would have adversely criticised.

Take 1 pumpkin of medium size
4 eggs, which beat well
1 small spoonful of salt
1 of ginger, ground
1 of cinnamon
1 cup of honey, which warm a little
½ cup of milk
½ cup of cream, whipped
A spoonful of vegetable oil

Prepare a pie crust to be baked. Cut the pumpkin in half, scraping out the seeds. Lightly oil the cut surface of the pumpkin halves which then place upside down in a pan lightly oiled, then bake until the flesh has become tender. Let stand a little while to cool as 'tis then too hot to handle. Scrape away the pumpkin flesh from the peel and make into a smooth pulp which some nowadays call purée.

Mix 2 cupfuls of the purée with the cinnamon and the ginger, then add into this the salt. Mix the beaten eggs with the honey and the milk and cream, which beat well and pour all into the pie shell.

This then is baked for some 50 minutes or until a knife slid close into the side of the pie comes back clean. Let this then cool and serve, pouring over it some of the whipped cream and lastly sprinkle over this a little of the cinnamon.

Glossary

Bushel: A measure of capacity containing 4 pecks or 8 gallons.

Caster: A small container with perforated holes in the lid, used for sprinkling sugar or spice, hence the term caster sugar.

Cock ale: Ale in which a rooster, usually an old one, has been boiled after being beaten and crushed with a heavy mallet; raisins and spices are added.

Great Cabin: The main cabin on board a warship used by the captain and senior officers.

Hogshead: A cask usually containing 54 imperial gallons.

Otaheite: Tahiti

Ramekin dish: A mould used to bake a mixture of cheese, breadcrumbs and eggs.

Salmi: A ragout of partly roasted game with wine and bread.

Saloop: A hot broth made from the root of an orchideous plant and later from sassafras, frequently on sale in the streets of London.

Sandalwood: Scented timber from the trees of the genus *Santalum*.

Scoter: A relatively large duck of the genus *Oedemia*, found in colder northern regions.

Spoonful: A small spoonful is usually known as a teaspoon, a spoonful as a tablespoon, and a large spoonful is roughly equivalent to a soup spoon.

Wort: The infusion of malt or grain which upon fermentation will produce beer; the term also refers to an infusion of malt used in the treatment of scurvy, ulcers and the like.

Bibliography

Beaglehole, John Cawte (ed.), *The Endeavour Journal of Joseph Banks 1768–1771*, 2 vols, Sydney, New South Wales, 1962.

Beaglehole, John Cawte (ed.), *The Journals of Captain James Cook on his Voyage of Discovery*, 3 vols, Cambridge, 1955–69.

Beaglehole, John Cawte, *The Life of Captain James Cook*, London, 1974.

David, Andrew, *et al.*, *The Malaspina Expedition 1789–1794*, 3 vols, London, 2001–4.

Day, Marelle, *Mrs Cook: The Real and Imagined Life of the Captain's Wife*, Crow's Nest, New South Wales, 2002.

Dunmore, John (ed.), *The Expedition of the St Jean-Baptiste to the Pacific 1769–1770*, London, 1981.

Dunmore, John (ed.), *The Journal of Jean-François de la Pérouse 1785–1786*, 2 vols, London, 1994.

Dunmore, John, (ed.), *The Pacific Journal of Louis-Antoine de Bougainville 1767–1768*, London, 2002.

Forster, Johann Georg Adam, *A Voyage Round the World in His Britannic Majesty's sloop* Resolution *commanded by Captain J. Cook, during the years 1772–1775*, 2 vols, London, 1777.

Forster, Johann Reinhold, *Observations made during a Voyage round the World*, London, 1778.

Fothergill, John, A *Complete Collection of the Medical and Philosophical Works of John Fothergill*, London, 1781.

Glasse, Hannah, *The Art of Cookery Made Plain and Easy*, 1747, reprinted London, 1983.

Hulme, Nathaniel, *Libellus de natura, causa curationeque Scorbuti, to which is annexed a Proposal for preventing the Scurvy in the British Navy*, London, 1768.

Hulme, Nathaniel, *A Safe and Easy Remedy proposed for the Relief of the Stone and Gravel, the Scurvy, Gout, &c*, London, 1778.

Lamb, W. Kaye (ed.), *The Voyage of George Vancouver 1791–1795*, 4 vols, London, 1984.

Lind, James, *A Treatise of the Scurvy*, Edinburgh, 1753.

Nott, John, *The Cook's and Confectioner's Dictionary*, London, 1726, reprinted London, 1980.

Rumford, Benjamin Thompson, Count, *Of Food, and Particularly of Feeding the Poor*, London, 1795; ed. R. Musgrave, Dublin, 1847.

Salmond, Anne, *The Trial of the Cannibal Dog: Captain Cook in the South Seas*, London, 2003.

Smith, Eliza, *The Compleat Housewife*, 1727, reprinted London, 1968.

Stead, Jennifer, *Food and Cooking in 18th Century Britain*, London, 1985.

Tannahill, Reay, *The Fine Art of Food*, London, 1968.

Trotter, Thomas, *Medica Nautica: An Essay on the Diseases of Seamen*, 2 vols, London, 1797–99.

Verral, William, *The Cook's Paradise*, 1759, reprinted London, 1948.

Wallis, Helen (ed.), *Carteret's Voyage Round the World 1766–1769*, 2 vols, Cambridge, 1965.

About the Author

John Dunmore retired as Professor of French at Massey University in 1983 after a distinguished academic career. A world authority on French navigation in the Pacific, he has written more than 20 books on the subject. His latest books are *Storms and Dreams*, a biography of Louis de Bougainville, and *Where Fate Beckons*, a biography of Jean-François de La Pérouse. Appointed a Companion of the New Zealand Order of Merit in 2001, Professor Dunmore was also made a knight of the Legion of Honour by the French Government in 1976.